TAX INSIGHT

FOR TAX YEAR 2013 AND BEYOND

SECOND EDITION

M. Casey Murdock

Apress

D1367259

Tax Insight: For Tax Year 2013 and Beyond

Copyright © 2013 by M. Casey Murdock

This work is subject to copyright. All rights are reserved by the Publisher, whether the whole or part of the material is concerned, specifically the rights of translation, reprinting, reuse of illustrations, recitation, broadcasting, reproduction on microfilms or in any other physical way, and transmission or information storage and retrieval, electronic adaptation, computer software, or by similar or dissimilar methodology now known or hereafter developed. Exempted from this legal reservation are brief excerpts in connection with reviews or scholarly analysis or material supplied specifically for the purpose of being entered and executed on a computer system, for exclusive use by the purchaser of the work. Duplication of this publication or parts thereof is permitted only under the provisions of the Copyright Law of the Publisher's location, in its current version, and permission for use must always be obtained from Springer. Permissions for use may be obtained through RightsLink at the Copyright Clearance Center. Violations are liable to prosecution under the respective Copyright Law.

ISBN-13 (pbk): 978-1-4302-6310-4

ISBN-13 (electronic): 978-1-4302-6311-1

Trademarked names, logos, and images may appear in this book. Rather than use a trademark symbol with every occurrence of a trademarked name, logo, or image we use the names, logos, and images only in an editorial fashion and to the benefit of the trademark owner, with no intention of infringement of the trademark.

The use in this publication of trade names, trademarks, service marks, and similar terms, even if they are not identified as such, is not to be taken as an expression of opinion as to whether or not they are subject to proprietary rights.

While the advice and information in this book are believed to be true and accurate at the date of publication, neither the authors nor the editors nor the publisher can accept any legal responsibility for any errors or omissions that may be made. The publisher makes no warranty, express or implied, with respect to the material contained herein.

President and Publisher: Paul Manning
Acquisitions Editor: Jeff Olson
Developmental Editor: Robert Hutchinson
Editorial Board: Steve Anglin, Mark Beckner, Ewan Buckingham, Gary Cornell, Louise Corrigan, Morgan Ertel, Jonathan Gennick, Jonathan Hassell, Robert Hutchinson, Michelle Lowman, James Markham, Matthew Moodie, Jeff Olson, Jeffrey Pepper, Douglas Pundick, Ben Renow-Clarke, Dominic Shakeshaft, Gwenan Spearing, Matt Wade, Tom Welsh
Coordinating Editor: Rita Fernando
Copy Editor: Terry Kornak
Compositor: SPi Global
Indexer: SPi Global
Cover Designer: Anna Ishchenko

Distributed to the book trade worldwide by Springer Science+Business Media New York, 233 Spring Street, 6th Floor, New York, NY 10013. Phone 1-800-SPRINGER, fax (201) 348-4505, e-mail orders-ny@springer-sbm.com, or visit www.springeronline.com. Apress Media, LLC is a California LLC and the sole member (owner) is Springer Science + Business Media Finance Inc (SSBM Finance Inc). SSBM Finance Inc is a Delaware corporation.

For information on translations, please e-mail rights@apress.com, or visit www.apress.com.

Apress and friends of ED books may be purchased in bulk for academic, corporate, or promotional use. eBook versions and licenses are also available for most titles. For more information, reference our Special Bulk Sales–eBook Licensing web page at www.apress.com/bulk-sales.

Any source code or other supplementary materials referenced by the author in this text is available to readers at www.apress.com. For detailed information about how to locate your book's source code, go to www.apress.com/source-code/.

Apress Business: The Unbiased Source of Business Information

Apress business books provide essential information and practical advice, each written for practitioners by recognized experts. Busy managers and professionals in all areas of the business world—and at all levels of technical sophistication—look to our books for the actionable ideas and tools they need to solve problems, update and enhance their professional skills, make their work lives easier, and capitalize on opportunity.

Whatever the topic on the business spectrum—entrepreneurship, finance, sales, marketing, management, regulation, information technology, among others—Apress has been praised for providing the objective information and unbiased advice you need to excel in your daily work life. Our authors have no axes to grind; they understand they have one job only—to deliver up-to-date, accurate information simply, concisely, and with deep insight that addresses the real needs of our readers.

It is increasingly hard to find information—whether in the news media, on the Internet, and now all too often in books—that is even-handed and has your best interests at heart. We therefore hope that you enjoy this book, which has been carefully crafted to meet our standards of quality and unbiased coverage.

We are always interested in your feedback or ideas for new titles. Perhaps you'd even like to write a book yourself. Whatever the case, reach out to us at editorial@apress.com and an editor will respond swiftly. Incidentally, at the back of this book, you will find a list of useful related titles. Please visit us at www.apress.com to sign up for newsletters and discounts on future purchases.

The Apress Business Team

I dedicate this book to you, the reader, for being courageous enough to delve into the thorny world of taxes, and savvy enough to recognize the need to do it. May you be well rewarded in this endeavor.

Contents

Foreword

An Awakening

Since 2004 I have been teaching people that they need a budget. They need to be aware. They need to plan and look ahead. They need to align their spending with their values and reach true financial contentment. Everything I teach encourages people to be forward focused.

When it comes to taxes, almost every one of us is facing backward. We look back and ask ourselves what we did last year to come up with what we pay. There is little to no planning.

We take our data, feed it into the black box (software, or those user-friendly IRS forms) and hope that what comes out on the other side is a "good" number. Hint: the only good number is the number you are legally obligated to pay—and not a penny more!

My awakening happened when Casey amended my 2008 business return and had me move a few things around only on paper that saved me more than $20,000 in taxes. I absolutely could not believe there was that much legitimate wiggle room inside the tax code. My savings had nothing to do with anything except how I reported my taxes. There was nothing fishy, gray, or shady in the way I revised my tax return. I simply sought and applied specialized knowledge to my specific situation—and it saved me a lot of money.

You have to be amused when people fret over the price of milk but turn a blind eye to their tax liability. With taxes, you're talking about the single largest expense of your life. Being smart with your taxes is the biggest win in the Big Win category.

Tax Insight: For Tax Year 2012 is not necessarily meant to be read cover to cover. Read the first five chapters and then pick the strategies that apply to your situation. You'll find it a fantastic reference going forward.

Jesse Mecham
Founder, YouNeedABudget.com

About the Author

M. Casey Murdock is a professional tax preparer, a financial advisor, and an enrolled agent with the IRS. He is also a co-owner of WealthGuard Advisors, Inc., where he leads the firm's tax practice.

Casey has a passion for minimizing taxes. It's the kind of thing you have to see for yourself to really understand. When he's working through your tax situation, he becomes transformed as he dials down into the deepest, darkest depths of the U.S. Tax Code. The only thing Casey enjoys more than reducing taxes is explaining how it is done. In *Tax Insight* he masterfully takes the ultra-complexity of the tax code and makes it easy to understand, using stories, examples, and simple explanations that he has developed as he has worked with his own tax clients over the years.

Casey would love to hear your feedback on the book. He is also open to discussing tax issues and strategies with you. If you would like to contact him, please do so by sending an e-mail to the following address: Casey@WealthGuardAdvisors.com.

Acknowledgments

I must begin by acknowledging and thanking Jesse Mecham for being the catalyst in the creation of this book. After his first tax experience with me, which he describes in the Foreword, he insisted that I should write a book. Then he promoted the self-published version for three years through his website, YouNeedABudget.com. Without his insistence I would never have considered such an audacious or presumptuous endeavor. Without his marketing prowess I would never have sold a single book. Without the sales in those first three years I would never have been noticed by my publisher. Thank you Jesse, for helping me turn a silly and whimsical idea (in my mind) into a reality that I still can't quite believe.

I also must acknowledge and thank my wonderful wife, Anna Marie, who has supported and encouraged me in more ways than I can list. There have been so many times when I wanted to stop and give up; so many times when I felt like it was ridiculous to write a book, or that no one would read it; so many times when I would have rather been home than be at my office before work, after work, and on Saturdays; so many times that it was hard for her to not have me home. But through it all she has kept me going and done it with hope and with a smile. On top of that, she has been the first to read each chapter I wrote and given me the feedback that I needed. This book would not exist without her continuous help, support, and encouragement.

I want to thank my eight wonderful children who have been so patient with their dad being gone; who have put off all of the things that they wanted to do with me; and whose prayers I have heard given in my behalf, and which have resulted in heaven's help.

I want to thank my cousin Trista, who has been unbelievably positive in her support. She has been a voice from outside my immediate circle of influence who has helped me believe that I could and should write this book.

Finally, I thank the people whom I have worked with at Apress. Thanks to Jeff Olson for taking notice of the book and being willing to make a run with it—even when I kept putting him off during tax season. Thanks to Robert Hutchinson for being gracious and kind throughout the editing process.

I really didn't know what it would be like to work with an editor, but his positive and helpful communications with me have set the bar high. I am also grateful to him for unabashedly using his expansive vocabulary, which has regularly led me to the dictionary in an effort to increase my own. Finally, thanks to Rita Fernando and others who have worked behind the scenes to bring the book to its final presentable form. You have all been great to work with and instrumental in bringing this book to print.

Introduction
Blackberries and Taxes: The Harvest Is Sweet

Picking wild blackberries is one of my family's favorite pastimes. In fact, blackberry season was at its peak in our area when I first had the inspiration for this book. One morning we were up early, picking to our hearts' content in a large blackberry patch near our home. As I was picking, I realized that the reason I love harvesting blackberries is very similar to the reason I love tax planning. Laugh if you will, but I think the same part of my brain is intrigued by both activities. For those who are not seasoned berry pickers, let me describe the experience.

Blackberry Picking

Wild blackberries are brambly, thorny plants. They emerge from long canes that reach in every direction and mesh together in a thorny maze. The thorns are sharp and curved, and they're particularly good at digging into your clothing and flesh as you try to pull away from them. In sharp contrast to the plant, however, the berries are heavenly. There is nothing more delicious than a ripe, juicy blackberry melting in your mouth.

The berries grow in clusters that are hidden throughout the blackberry bush. In fact, each bush conceals significantly more berries than those you see at first glance. Finding the hidden clusters of berries, without getting hurt by the thorns, is both challenging and rewarding. It is in that challenge that you find both the art and the intrigue of berry picking.

The casual berry picker often finds a few tasty treats easily within his reach on every berry bush. However, the taste of one sour berry, or a good jab from a thorn, is usually enough to deter the casual picker from making further efforts. He is not willing to deal with the thorns, the tearing of flesh and clothes, and other obstacles in the way of obtaining berries deeper in the bush. He is content to just get a little taste and then move on.

In contrast, the serious berry picker is not deterred by such obstacles. In fact, she develops a method through years of practice that inevitably yields larger, juicier fruits—as well as much greater quantities of berries. Here is how she does it.

She begins with a berry bush that has several nice-looking berries hanging right out on the edge of the plant. No berry picker would ever pass these up. As she picks all the ripe fruit from the clumps within reach, she begins to notice other clusters (better than the ones before) that are just out of reach. So, the serious picker presses into the thorny bush and reaches in as far as she can, careful to avoid the thorns. As she reaches in deep and picks the juicy delights, her arm brushes against other branches, which then reveal a treasure trove of once-hidden berries.

Seeing her efforts rewarded, she won't be stopped as she digs her way right into the middle of the bush. Thorns threaten at every move, but the reward is too great for these obstacles to deter her. She makes her way through the brambles and fills her baskets to overflowing. As she looks around for more berries, it appears that she has picked all of the ripe fruit. As she works her way back out of the bush she sees a berry she had missed and squats down to pick it up. From her new perspective she sees a dozen other clusters that she couldn't see before. She'll soon be back with more baskets to continue her harvest.

In this way the serious berry picker harvests the larger, sweeter berries, and in much greater quantity than the casual picker. The experienced picker knows that berries are hiding everywhere. Every bush must be explored from every angle—each thorny branch moved to reveal what lies beneath.

Taxberries

Picking berries is similar to preparing taxes. Certain "berries" (deductions and credits) are visible to nearly everyone. Many people take advantage of these and taste the sweet reward of saving a few tax dollars. However, most people are unwilling to trudge deeper into the thorny world of taxes to discover additional unseen yet juicy fruits. The confusing bramble of the tax code discourages them from entering. The ever-present, always looming thorns of IRS audits and penalties elicit too much fear of pain to justify reaching for the berries—especially among people who are inexperienced in avoiding those thorns. Even for those few who are willing to make the effort, many "clusters" of berries are certain to be missed, and thorns are certain to be felt, without the help of more experienced eyes.

The good news for casual pickers is that there are people who have a passion for "taxberry" picking. They are unafraid to trudge into the brambles to find every hidden berry. Better still, these passionate pickers are willing to be hired to pick your taxberry bush for you, or write how-to books like this one.

As you read this book, you will find me digging deep into the brambles of your taxberry bush, holding up the branches and showing you the fruit. I will also point out the thorns. I will teach you how to nurture and fertilize the plant. As you follow my lead you will reap the rewards of a plentiful harvest.